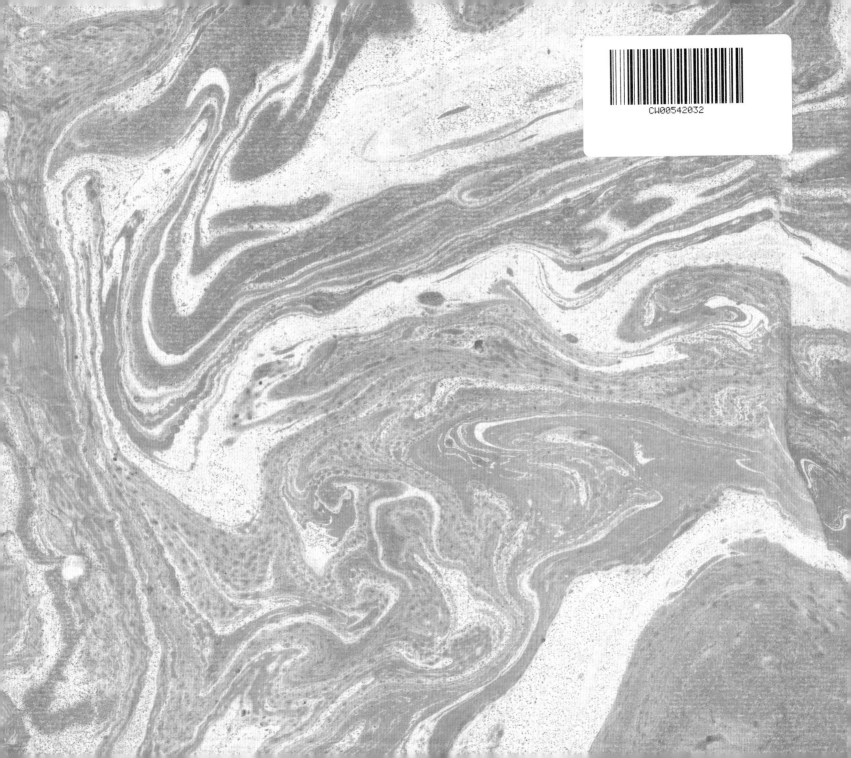

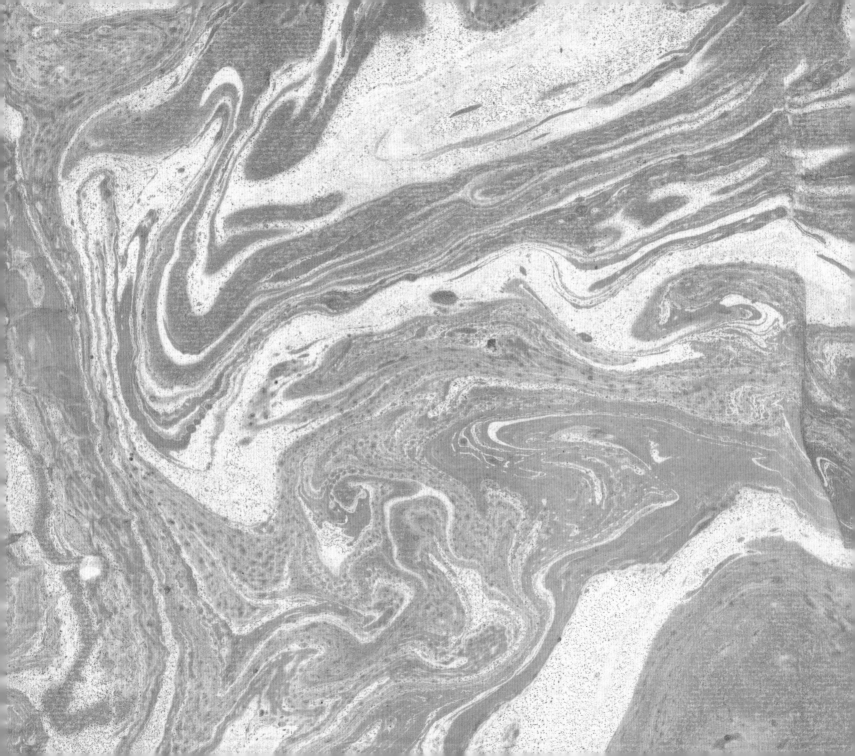

FOR OUR GOOD FRIEND JIM RUSSELL
TRUE GENTLEMAN, FINE ARTIST, KINDLY TEACHER
AND LOYAL SUPPORTER OF THE WINE SOCIETY
THIS BOOK IS DEDICATED TO HIS MEMORY.

"JOIE DE VIVRE LIES BETWEEN RUE DE
WAKENING AND RUE MATISME"

(GASTON DUPLONK,
1886–)

With All Good wishes from
Graham Clarke

VINI VINI VINI

VINERELLES
VIGNETTES &
VILE VERSES VERITABLE
PAR
Graham Clarke

72 PAGES

NONE GENUINE WITHOUT THIS SIGNATURE
(DEPUIS 1941)

100% PROOF READ

EBENEZER PRESS
2005

Sincere thanks to good friends at the Wine Society for providing me with dregs of many fine wines in order to produce the images and lettering for this book. I called them dregs but they told me it would be better to call them lees – quite right too.

Also grateful thanks to Grant Bradford (*book wizard*), 'Printing Professor' Roger Multon; any amount of clever people that I don't know but who helped to produce this volume, and my dear wife Wendy, who makes indulgences such as this possible.

First published in 2005 by EBENEZER PRESS the Imprint of Graham Clarke Limited, White Cottage, Green Lane, Boughton Monchelsea, Maidstone, Kent, ME17 4LF, U.K.

Telephone: 01622 743938 Facsimile: 01622 747229
E.mail: info@grahamclarke.co.uk
Website: www.grahamclarke.co.uk

Colour Reproduction by Redkifree Graphic Arts, Hong Kong.
Printed by Yiu Cheong Printing & Binding, China

ISBN No. 0-9502357-4-1

WATER INTO WINE AND VICE VERSA

The absent-minded artist's life is not without its hazards and drinking one's paint water is certainly one of them. It is most likely to happen when deeply absorbed in one's task but have a drink on hand for fortification, perhaps a mug of coffee or cocoa or in this artist's case, possibly a glass of wine.

Paint water unsullied by the more dangerous pigments of the palette is little more than an unwelcome surprise, but you don't need too much cadmium red or cobalt blue to make you feel distinctly 'off colour'. It is worse still for oil painters of course, some of whom, especially the French Impressionists and Impersonists on absinthe have been known to swig a litre of dirty turps before realising their mistake, part of the reason why there are so few of them wielding the brush nowadays one might suppose.

The lesson to be learned is this, don't place your restorative beverage anywhere near the water pot. Putting them on opposite sides of your easel or drawing board can dramatically cut the accident rate. An obvious rule but seldom taught in art colleges, even in this age of institutional health and safety.

For red wine drinkers there is a special danger when working with Alizarin Crimson, particularly if both vessels are made of glass, so an opaque water pot is highly recommended. Apart from drinking one's paint water the other and more dismal hazard is to ruin a decent glass of wine by sticking a dirty brush in it, again easily done even by the most accomplished practitioners.

Exactly how many times I plonked my No. 4 Winsor and Newton genuine Kolinsky sable into the glass of modest Argentine Malbec, I have no idea, but the resulting 'aquarelle' (as the French insist on calling watercolours) seemed to exude a pleasing warmth. I only realised what I had been doing when upon completion, to my astonishment the water pot still contained pure clear water. In a moment of uncharacteristic restraint I did not quaff the Malbec as it had turned an interesting shade of Khaki.

Our ink critic writes:-

"Amply demonstrating the dedicated contemporary wine boiler's skills, exuding an exotic savour of pickled beetroot aromas with modest stewed apricot and broccoli overtones, combined in perfect balance conveying the classic hint of a Harry Ramsden vinegar dispenser with an intensely pleasing lack of tropical fruit flavours and freshly cut grass, nevertheless it attempts to amuse with a marvellously rubicund Gallic nose of considerable complexity proving a viticultural abomination of prodigious redolence."

As is often said of cheap red wines by amateur experts, "It's just like red ink". You may like to know that much of the red ink used in this little book to letter the original text is made from the lees or dregs of Château Palmer 1988 the remains of two magnums of the lovely stuff. 'Mis en bouteille au château' as they say but boiled down in my kitchen. For even a richly coloured red wine gives only the palest of pinks when applied with a steel pen nib or sable brush it must be reduced to about a tenth of the original volume to be anywhere near satisfactory, and smells wonderful in so doing, quite redolent in fact.

10.

How marvellously proud we should all be to find this piscatorial tribute
to British seafaring prowess in many a French supermarket.

Rue de l'Horloge in beautiful Alba La Romaine in the Ardèche, nearby live our dear friends Marie-Françoise and Maurice Arlaud, Maurice is a vigneron and past Master of the Confrèrie des Chevaliers du Cep Ardèchois. In an uncharacteristically rash moment he invited me to become a Chevalier.
"Oui" I answered a millionth of a second later.

UN REPAS SANS VIN C'EST COMME UNE FLEUR SANS PARFUM.

← CARRELET

These wonderful dip-net fishing machines stride
along the estuary of the Gironde and I love them.
They probably don't make the fishermen very
prosperous but they must be safer and much
more comfortable than a wobbly old boat.

Across the still waters lies the Medoc the flat
undramatic land that produces many of the
world's greatest wines. A drop or two of Château
Palmer 1997 would 'go down a treat' with a decent
bit of haddock and chips but then I'm a heretic.

LA ROCHE

A tiny vineyard almost in the lovely square of La Roche, dominated and named after the monstrous plug of an ancient volcano. Just up the hill is wonderful, dusty, crumbling Alba la Romaine, capital of all the surrounding area in Roman times it even has a Roman theatre to prove it.

I cannot claim to be the first artist to use wine as a painting medium for use with watercolours either by accident or interest. However, I have never heard of the works thus produced being referred to as "Vinerelles" before. Perhaps I am the first to intensify the colour by boiling red wine down for use as ink but I suspect not, wine and writing have been in close company for too long for them not to have been employed in this way before.

The marbled end papers were produced using traditional oil colours floated on three bottles of "El cheapo" red, a grape based beverage definitely not to be found in the lists of the excellent Wine Society.

TAILLE D'HIVER

Winter pruning, traditionally begun on St. Vincent's Day, 22nd January.

16

Husband and wife hard at work in their cosy
little 'French Café' in Saga City, Kyushu, Japan.
And a very satisfactory lunch was had by all.

The Japanese are modest concerning their
domestic wines but they've been making them
for a very long time and the best are excellent
and expensive. They believe however that I can
only drink "posh names" from France.
Accordingly, one morning around 10am two
young men in evening dress entered one of my
exhibitions in Osaka pushing a large silver plated
trolley smothered with crisp white napkins. They
presented me with an excellent and venerable
red claret. Such a shame about the ice bucket.

Don't worry about the jars of chopsticks

VILE VERSES VERTITABLE

Dear reader,
The verses appearing in this book include my
failed entries for the Wine Society Limerick
Competition of Christmas 2003, I had hoped
to be enthroned as the Society's Poet Limerate.

My grandpa was quite fond of sherry
In fact you could say he was very
But gentleman he
Drunk just two or three
So seldom got more than just merry

To scribble a limerick's fine
Especially if it's about wine
But our good Wine Society
Is all for propriety
So I'm not too sure about mine

Muscadet (Wine Socs.) sur lie
Costs more or less four ninety-three
With all kinds of dishes
But specially fishes
It surely sur lie pleases me

Your Sebastian Master of Wine
Sorts out the turps from the fine
I don't want to trouble you
And I'm not an M.W.
But could we swap his job for mine?

I once drunk some Clairette de Die
With my gizzards it didn't agree
A kind friend of mine
(he's a master of wine)
Said, "Need to pass wind? Please feel free"

I study those excellent lists
And grab any bargains I've missed
From Bordeaux to the Var
And the Rhone to the Loire
So I know I can really get pretty
good value for money

Your phylloxera beetle is evil
He'll chew at the roots and he'll leav'all
The vines looking dead
As the Vigneron said
"Zat beetle's ze trés evil weevil"

LABOURAGE

March, ploughing between the rows to aerate the soil and expose the bases of the vines.

Carole Lamont diligently tends her 5 acres of Bacchus Reichensteiner and Pinot Noir. Clay Hills Vineyard on the Kent Sussex border in the Teise Valley next to Bayham Abbey the most beautiful setting in England?

Tokyo Kushikatsu chefs on the job. Everything is fried on little wooden skewers, thirty or more courses of dainty delicacies from asparagus to ducks gizzards. They will keep feeding you until you can take no more, so you must inform them of your intention to cease eating two or three sticks in advance.

Put your used skewers in the mouth of a nice ceramic fish, these when added up are your bill.

Legend has it that one gentleman worked his way through the entire menu sequence three times plus a few more but just failed to make the century, it is not recorded how many fishes were required for his sticks.

Exact details of the incident portrayed opposite are not known, for example what is the central figure doing looking at his bottle with such intensity, why is he wearing co-respondents shoes and seafarers cap and why does his colleague behind the barrel look so dismal. Is the lady in the pink coat his wife, sister or disapproving aunt and if not, why not.
Of one thing you can be sure however, the sky was painted with Winsor & Newtons French Ultramarine mixed with Hermitage '88 La Chapelle of Paul Jaboulet Aîné.

CHEZ GASTON

Our English diners have waited long and most patiently for lunch to arrive. Nobly demonstrating sang froid, esprit de coeur, savoir faire and a great deal of noblesse obilge.

What a pity then that Gaston, who owing to the staff shortage decided he should serve them himself, is about to trip over the restaurant cat.

28

Though evidence is of course scanty
One's instincts inform one that Dante
Whilst on his Inferno
Didn't drink Pernod
More likely the local Chianti

Drinks delivery on the Grand Canal in wonderful Venice, a noisy and interesting spectacle inducing much animated excitement amongst the noble delivery men no doubt with a resulting thirst.

One of the several establishments being supplied is Antica Carbonera just around the corner in Calle Carbon. The proprietor is Umberto, an elderly most distinguished gentleman of great perception – he likes my pictures and puts them in his restaurant window, he doesn't actually pay for them with money, I just sort of eat them for him.

"But Gaston you told me you liked my fish soup".

"That was 35 years ago Francine my dear".

The winemaking name of Laroche
Is famous and really quite posh
For that special dinner
Their Chablis' a winner
So swig posh Laroche with your nosh

33

ECLAIRCIR

**After the vines have flowered at the beginning of June,
thin the shoots and tie the best of them to the wires.**

PETIT GRANGE, ALBA

A kilometre or so out of Alba La
Romaine my good friend Maurice has
his ancient and prolific cherry orchard.
Scene of many a joyful cherry red-
handed stone-spitting picnic. Artists
are not expected to pick so I take a
little time off to record old Gaston and
his six rows of vines just down the lane.

The Pirate sailed nearer and nearer
Intentions got clearer and clearer
We had dreadful qualms'e
Was after our Malmsey
So we swigged all the skippers Madeira

The painter takes a few slurps
Then finds he's been swigging his turps
Drops all his brushes
To doctor he rushes
Who bravely sets fire to the burps

My wife is quite fond of fizz
In fact she thinks its 'the bizz'
"How's the bouquet?
Sure it's o.k.?"
She invariably answers "It is"

Of all the cultural shocks that lay in wait for the green and pleasant young English gentleman surely it was the terra cotta tyres on the creaking bicycles of the malodorous old French gaffers.

GASTON DuPLONK

DOGMATISME

The scrofulous cur beneath the handsome saucisson vendor's Sunday Market stall is Gonzalo, the canine Ghengis Khan of Alba La Romaine. Make a purchase and if you are fortunate he will merely nip your leg. The stallholder to whom he does not belong once made the mistake of giving him a piece of sausage, he and his customers are still paying the price.

Mad Frenchman swigs too much champagne
Gets plastered in Paris again
With knees all a quiver
He falls in the river
And thereby is proven in Seine

PAGE
41

LE CLUB BOUILLABAISSE

ENTRÉE LIBRE

I enjoy making my version of Bouillabaisse which I call Bait Box Stew. It requires only $2/3$ bottle of El Cheapo Red or Priceless Claret amongst its ingredients thus neatly rendering a couple of glasses for the 'chef' before the guests arrive. When the bottle is empty taste your stew and decide that it really could do with rather more wine after all and open another bottle – and so on.

(From The Devout Fish Gluttons Handbook by George Ivor Dunnet)

VILE VERSES AGAIN

Likes a drink does my good friend Roger
A thoroughly decent old codger
A real nice fella
But if you've got a cellar
I wouldn't have him as a lodger

French waitress said "Monsieur pardonez
Would sir like a glass of Chardonnay?"
I'm not keen on tots
But far prefer lots
So the whole bloomin' case she m`a donné

"Just a tiny drop dear" she'd say
My auntie of her Dubonnet
She rhymed it with sonnet
Not Monet but bonnet
In her anglisised auntified way

Using the bosses best Margaux
New chef stews a dozen escargots
Boss said "the pud
Had better be good
Or I'll boot your backside and you'll far go"

PULVÉRISATION

July, spray regularly with Bordeaux mixture against the oidiums (maladie de la vigne) the dreaded mildew.

MONTFLEURIE
OR SPELT MORE CORRECTLY
MONTFLEURY

Less than a hamlet just a derelict railway station, a bit of a river but only in winter and the roadside Auberge where I ate the strongest smelliest piece of cheese the world has ever known, also a splendid Cave Cooperative to look after the vignerons and this pleasant farm with it's vineyard on its 'flowery hill'.

Though pinching his father's best port
The young rascal seldom got caught
It wasn't my brother
So must be some other
Yours truly? Oh perish the thought

The village square of Ste. Croix way up the
beautiful valley carved by the river Drôme.
The extraordinary church is divided into two,
each with it's own tower, one half for the
Catholics and the other for the Protestants.
Differences put aside no doubt they both agree
upon the excellence of the sparkling Clairette
de Die produced a few kilometres further up
the gorge.

VILE VERSES

A friend has a cellar that's chocka-
block full of rioja
If thieves try again
To return it to Spain
He'll have to remember to lioja

I know a trombonist who has
A passion for Aussie Shiraz
He confesses a little
Is wasted in spittle
Can't be helped when he plays all that jazz

At one time it might have seemed silly
For fine wines to reach us from Chile
But the fact that they're nice
And a reasonable price
Means now they arrive willy-nilly

From the Ruwer the Mosel and Rhine
They produce some wonderful wine
But I fear it has taken some time
To find a suitable rhyme
For Eitelsbacher Karthäuserhofberg Reisling
Kabinett, Iphöfer Krönsberg Silvaner Spätlese
Trocken or Reisling Zöbinger Herligenstein

It's a good time to buy Argentina
As prices have never been keener
Its excellent stuff
And not a bit rough
A better time there's hardly been a

This truly is one of the oldest areas of wine production in the world and it is just possible that Jonah really did drink a distant ancestor of the famous and much respected Chateau Musar of today.

The best known powerful red wine from the Lebanon. Highly spiced with amazing keeping properties, note the date on the label.

MID 8th CENTURY B.C.

MARQUE   DÉPOSÉE

LABOR OMNIA VINCIT

Chateau Musar

★

GASTON HOCHAR
PROPRIÉTAIRE VITICULTURE - GHAZIR - LIBAN

MIS EN BOUTEILLES AU CHATEAU

PRODUCE OF LEBANON / BEKAA VALLEY

13% vol   75cl

2 KINGS 14·25

And the Lord Preparerd A Great Fish
(Jonah Ch. 1 v. 17.)
He even remembered the corkscrew.
Chateau Musar
Chateau Musar
Chateau Musar

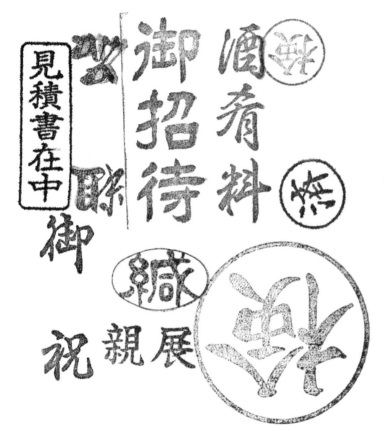

DRY OLD DO

How we love the Japanese bullet trains, so fast, so clean and always exactly on time with a nice little shop somewhere around car no. 8 or 9 to buy our lunch. On this occasion pieces of fried chicken on sticks, octopus chunks with a little salad and fish eggs in cold rice wrapped in a seaweed parcel, all very dainty. A bit too dainty were the bottles of Zinfandel Californian so called 'white', nothing exactly wrong with it except the size of the bottle. We achieved the doubtful honour of drinking the entire train dry, not such a remarkable feat as there were only a couple of 25cl plastic bottles of it to begin with.

心をこめて…

A Light Lunch on the
Shinkansen

酒肴料

VENDANGER, *oops!*

September
Pray for good weather then pick your grapes.

COLOMBIER -MIRABEL

Half way down the Rhone valley lies the nougat capital of the entire universe, Montelimar, an ideal place to purchase a little something to take home for your dentist.

Turn right (West) and you enter the wild and beautiful Ardeche, once famous for silk and chestnuts now it's reputation grows year by year for good quality modestly priced wines.

I know, my friends make them*
*This won't do me any harm eh?

TEPANYAKI

Tepanyaki chefs, our good friend Mr. Sakaguchi on the left preparing our dinner. Both Chablis and Cognac are sploshed on to the meat or fish during their brief spell on the hot plate.

Beef, fish and vegetables are meticulously prepared in the kitchens and dissected with expertise and precision for brisk cooking before our very eyes on the thick steel 'tepan'. This is edible theatre.

It seems Pete, perched on the harbourside in Corfu, does not have a modesty problem and if he really does have the best prices in town and is recommended world wide and indeed was the first person to introduce pizzas to his island, who can blame him.

A handsome young Greek window cleaner
Peeped in a taverna and seen a...
Girl getting dressed
And was greatly impressed
So ordered spiced lamb and Retsina

A fine little statue of a very great man along the lane between the famous Burgurdian wine villages of Aloxe Corton and Pernand Vergelesses.
He holds a large pruning knife in one hand and a bunch of grapes in the other and was in his day Emperor of most of Europe. Interestingly his father's name was Pepin III the Short. Pip Pip Pip Pop.

To a faraway vineyard we'd walked
For a Burgundy out we had forked
Such a long traipse
Just to get some squashed grapes
And when we got back it was corked

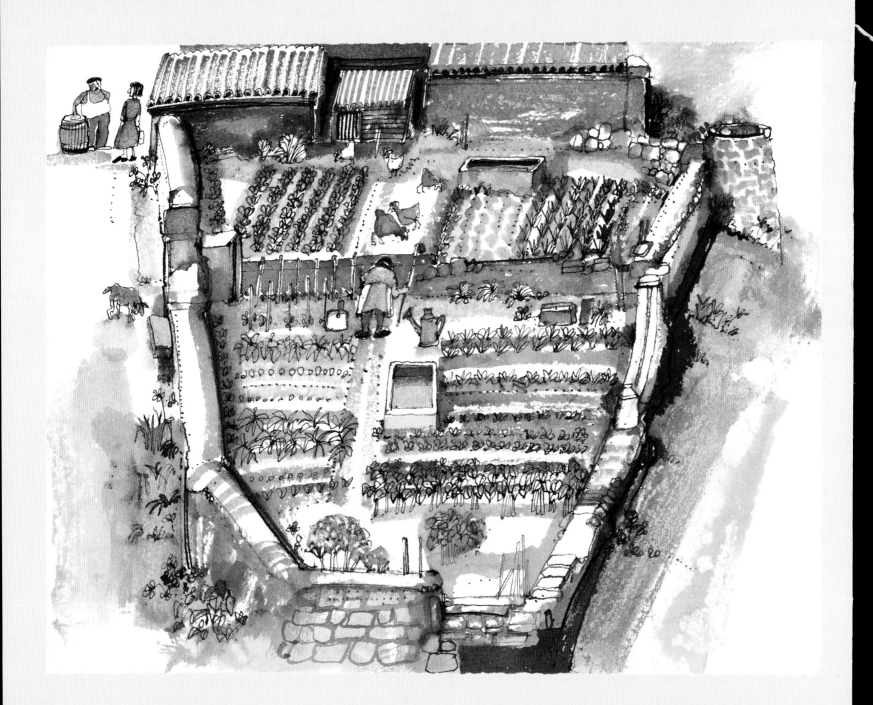

Beautiful walled gardens below the ancient
bridge in Vogüé, Ardeche. To the right is the
river, tranquil when the weather has been
kind with sandy beaches as perfect as any
by the seaside.

To the left the village itself, a tightly packed
marvellous disorganisation of crumbly buildings.
Above them towers the fine Château where one
wonderful evening in 1993 I was 'introniser'
Chevalier in the 'jardin suspendu' to the sound
of trumpets with food provided by the President
of the Lady Chefs of France. Noblesse Obilge
as we say in Kent.

They asked how would you like to be
Chevalier in our confrèrie?
With flat hat and cloak
I'm a very proud bloke
Proud bloke in the cloak now that's me

FERMENTATION

**Skilled work in the cave, the new wine is fermenting,
last years can be given it's final racking.**

Dégustation obligatoire
Gaston approves

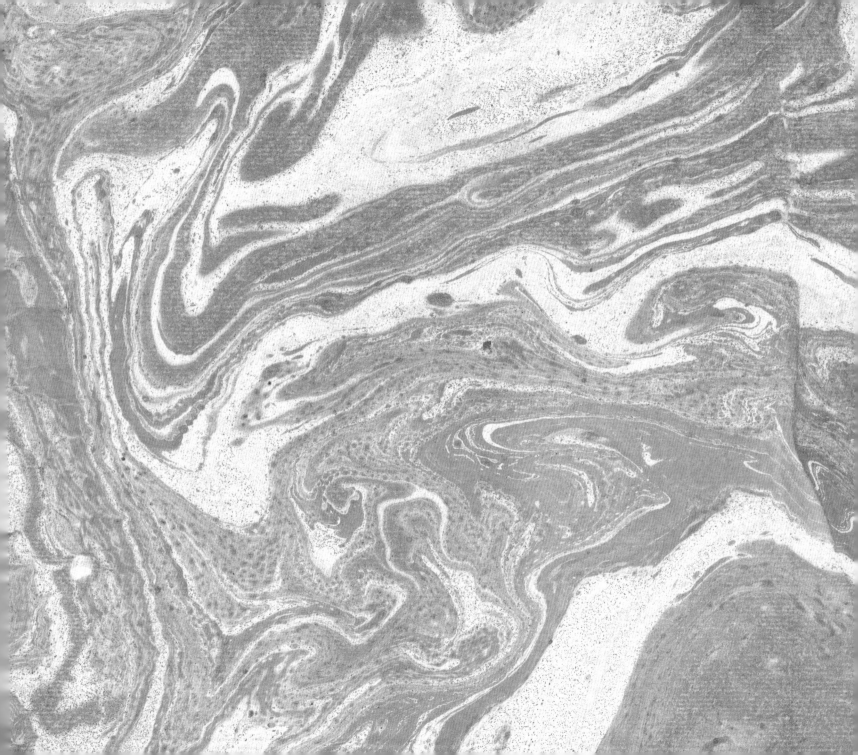

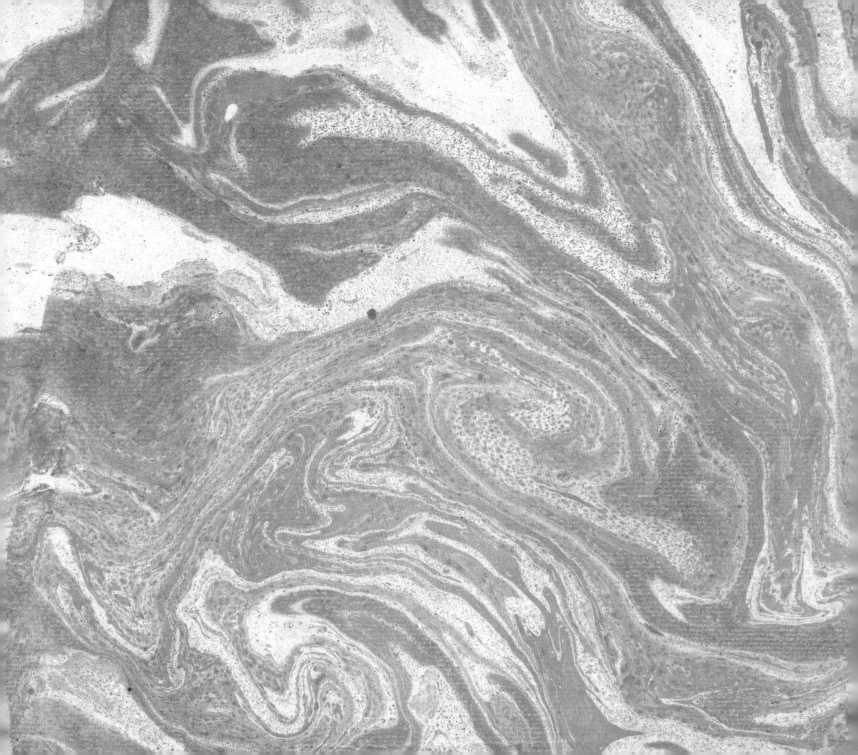